*For my grandmother, Leap...*
*i.m. 1932–2020*

## A Thousand Crimson Blooms

Eileen Chong is an Australian poet of Chinese descent. She was born and raised in Singapore, and came to Australia as an adult migrant. She started writing poetry in 2010, and is the author of eight books published in Australia and the United States. Her work has been shortlisted for numerous prizes, such as the Anne Elder Award, the Australian Arts in Asia Award, the NSW Premier's Literary Award, the Victorian Premier's Literary Award, and twice for the Prime Minister's Literary Award. Her first book, *Burning Rice*, is the first single-author collection of poetry by an Asian-Australian to be studied as part of the NSW HSC English syllabus. She lives and works on unceded Gadigal land of the Eora Nation. eileenchong.com.au

## Also by Eileen Chong

# Eileen **Chong**

## A Thousand Crimson Blooms

UQP

First published 2021 by University of Queensland Press
PO Box 6042, St Lucia, Queensland 4067 Australia
Reprinted 2021

University of Queensland Press (UQP) acknowledges the Traditional Owners and
their custodianship of the lands on which UQP operates. We pay our respects to their
Ancestors and their descendants, who continue cultural and spiritual connections to
Country. We recognise their valuable contributions to Australian and global society.

uqp.com.au
reception@uqp.com.au

Cover design by Sandy Cull, gogoGingko
Author photograph by Charlene Winfred Photography
Typeset in 11.5/14 pt Bembo Std by Post Pre-press Group, Brisbane
Printed in Australia by McPherson's Printing Group

University of Queensland Press is assisted
by the Australian Government through
the Australia Council, its arts funding and
advisory body.

A catalogue record for this book is available from the National Library of Australia.

ISBN 978 0 7022 6319 4 (pbk)
ISBN 978 0 7022 6493 1 (epdf)

University of Queensland Press uses papers that are natural, renewable and recyclable
products made from wood grown in well-managed forests and other controlled
sources. The logging and manufacturing processes conform to the environmental
regulations of the country of origin.

MIX
Paper from
responsible sources
FSC® C001695

# Contents

## The Hymen Diaries

## Griefs

## Sweet Truth

## Singapore Koel

*for Charlene Winfred*

In the land of our birth,
we wander by winding waterways,
measuring this parched earth—

We know our time will end.
Dusk descends. Denouement of days:
a parting, once more, of friends.

# Paper Boats

# In My Fortieth Year, I Realise I Am Not Them

The moon rises above clouds.
In the cold light, all is grey, and white.

Night sky turns on a paper wheel.
Stars are silvered, immutable.

The only sound: a deer scarer
filling, emptying, and filling again.

忍

You whet a knife,
press the edge to my
heart. You draw blood—

I breathe from the centre
of my being, so my chest
betrays no rise and fall. I hold

still. I look for the moon,
but tonight, there are only clouds.
Today, a new word: *thole*—to endure

what is barely bearable. I
will have to do this my entire life.
Like my mother and father before

me; their mothers and fathers
before them. We know this word.
I bite my tongue. I write it, red on white.

# A Thousand Crimson Blooms

*Look here, children —*
*There by your feet,*
*A tiny, yellow flower!*
        'Don't Trample This Flower', Bing Xin

Little ones, let's put pencil to paper,
draw the backyard rooster, sketch your loyal dog:
one to announce daybreak, the other to watch all night.

Let's shape their bodies with our hands.
Let's gouge out cavities with our fingers.
We are a hundred lidless eyes.

★

You there—go out into the desert.
Come back when you've stopped weeping.
Who shall we drown in glass today?
Who will withstand the flames?

The blue-and-white vases are broken.
They made us walk across the shards.
Our cut feet are a thousand crimson blooms.
It's certain death for flowers without roots.

# Dog Meals

The dead women always fed me.
In their kitchens, water ran from brass taps,
next to thick wooden chopping blocks
where cleavers lay glistening—

bowls of sliced pork belly braised in soy,
trembling with fat; plates of wok-seared rice
fried to a near-crisp with onion and garlic;
cabbage, black fungus and beancurd skins

stewed with glass noodles and dried shrimp.
I have eaten these willingly. The last woman
to die consumed three whole meals of the new
dog year before she laid her head down in the dark,

never to wake again to brew strong coffee
with condensed milk, to spread kaya on toast,
to crack open soft-boiled eggs. Nothing left but
a procession of black ants crawling across the counter.

# Rainbow

On the first day, we ate the trout
with its skin on. Scales in my teeth.
You said: let the knife do the work.

★

The second day, I laid the fish out
on its side; I pinched its edge and slid
the blade clean between fat and muscle.

★

Not all rainbow: here, tender orange,
there, rusted brown, the underside
gelatinous and white. Then the bones.

★

Over lunch, the man and woman
carved fillets from each other
one word at a time.

★

The cat licks remnants of flesh
from flayed skin. Its tongue:
red, methodical, and barbed.

★

Nothing left for the third day
save the offcuts. Cubes of cured
trout layered on pickles and rice.

★

How to multiply one fish into many—
my mother ties an unseen knot. The string
is invisible. Yet the hooked fish pulls.

# Courage

I pour out my troubles to my mother.
Our coffees: black, and white.

吓到了, she clucks. *You've taken fright.*
A mouth turned downwards, an arrival,

an exhalation of breath, a sound of finality.
We lift the cups to our lips, then lower them

onto their saucers. *I want to tell you,* I begin,
but I cannot find the words. I remember

to ask her questions. *I'm sorry to tell you this,*
as she shows me a video of her mother

struggling to stand. I cry; I am afraid
my grandmother will fall; I am afraid

we will all fail. I fell once—hanging
from the monkey bars, my weight proved

too much for my grip. Sand and skin
are incompatible. Rawness and blood.

In the school office, the secretary
dabbed at my scrapes with iodine;

I returned to the classroom wearing
the purple smudge of courage.

We drain our coffees much too fast.
We do not like anything served cold.

Where do we find the strength?
Who will speak our names in the night?

Her bus is on time. She clutches
at the handrail and pulls herself up

each step, laboriously. I wait for her
to find a seat, for her to turn towards

me. She waves at me, and I return her wave.
The bus moves. Her face becomes a blur.

# Teacher

*after Jenny Xie's 'Naturalization'*

My mother tells everyone I am a *cheecher*,
she never knows how to say *poet*, or *writer*.

I pour her some tea, hand her a mug,
and point at it. She says *TEAcher*,

I say *TEAcher*, then, I say *teacher*.
I teach her; I feel like an arsehole.

Like the time two kids pushed her
off the footpath because she walked

down the middle. I pulled her back up;
I told them, *You should be ashamed of yourselves.*

I told her, *Keep to the left. You take up so much
space.* I was angry. She was ashamed.

We are sitting on the floor. She is passing
one end of a shoelace through a loop;

she pulls, and miraculously, it tightens.
We are counting coins; she says, *Here*

*is a dollar: this one is a fifty, these two
are twenties, this one, a ten.* We are standing

at the bus stop. She says, *When the bus
turns left at the big red house, get up, push*

*the bell, and get off.* My mother is telling me
about her art class. Her teacher said,

*I don't understand what you are saying.* I pour
my mother more tea; I offer and cut her

a slice of lemon cake. I tell her, *She's not
listening to you.* The cake is sweet, despite

its sourness. Today, she has painted a stag.
She points at it: *this leg missing, like no leg.*

The trees are dense in our forest. Three
legs make a tripod. The kettle is in the flames;

the tea leaves are waiting to be read. I pick
at all the knots. I am adding up to a whole.

# My Mother, Painting

My mother sends me an image
of her painting for the week. I reply:
*I think the original will be hard to beat.*

She spends hours copying masterpieces:
Hopper's lighthouse, Smithson's spiral,
Da Vinci's Mona Lisa. When I got married,

she gave us a likeness of me, aged three,
sitting along the five-foot-way outside
our shophouse on Victoria Street.

She didn't like it. *I couldn't get your face right.*
There's only a blur of beige with pale lips
and dark eyes. My feet are suspended;

I was swinging my legs. She's painted in
the motorbike belonging to the man
who welded metal bars. Fire sparking

across the pavement; the iron-rich stench
of hot steel. Inside the office, someone
strokes me in the darkness when I hide

under the table. The orange lamps of the altar
burn like witnesses; incense blankets
the air. A finger is pressed across my lips.

Later, in the kitchen, I suck on a lemon lolly
and I imagine getting more. Bruises
on my thighs. Take up the brush—Prussian

blue, vermilion red. Yet the paint has dried;
the painting is framed. My mother cannot
craft in art what she never saw in life.

# Hunger

I have told the story often—I see her:
nine years old, a tangle of unruly hair, standing on a chair
to reach the pot over the heat. She was five when
she learned to strike a match, to ignite a fire-starter,
how to coax a red-hot glow from charcoal in the stove.

Outside the kitchen, the other children are playing:
a boundary drawn with a stick of chalk, solid globes chipped upon
impact. Games of skill and cunning; knowing just how much force
to use to swing and lob a glass ball so it would smash into another,
edging it across the finish line. Tiny wars waged for whole worlds that clatter.

In the dark recess of the shophouse, dim with a single
strip of cold light mounted on the wall with peeling paint,
rice is burning in the pot. The chair has been abandoned;
my mother is watching her brothers win another bag of marbles.
Her mother will soon descend the stair. Then beat her. They will all hunger.

# Fortune-Telling

*All night I dreamed of my home,*
*of the roads that are so long*
*and straight they die in the middle—*
                    'Signs', Larry Levis

When I was fifteen a fortune-teller examined
my palm and fell silent. My grandmother
murmured under her breath, in their language.
He turned my hand this way, then that—

I was not to marry young; tragedy lay ahead.
Did I listen? Wild as a weed that grows in a crack
in the pavement. The life line bifurcated, the heart
line split. No children, maybe two; a boy, certainly,

perhaps a girl, with dark hair. I never saw their faces.
When I was six a teacher taped my mouth shut because
my soul kept trying to sing at all the wrong times.
I soon learned what *No* meant, and I would learn it again

and again. At twenty-four, they cut a lump
from my neck; at thirty-seven, another from my arm.
My skin would tear away with each new dressing. A clean
wound heals. Scars like lidless eyes, helpless and watching.

# My Mother Talks in Numbers

*What is home?*
Forty years of morning, noon, and night.

*Tell me about your childhood.*
Thirty-seven mouths open under a tin roof.

*What is happiness?*
Eighteen in my sailor suit, spray from the waterfall—

*Why did you marry?*
Five years of coins.

*How many tears?*
One thousand, eight hundred, and ninety-eight pearls.

*Did you love your mother?*
Two hands, ten fingers, six children.

*How many miles have you come?*
Sixty-four thousand and twenty-five gull-wings.

*Do you love me?*
The rain falling, falling, over thirteen thousand dawns.

# A New Year

Another birthday come and gone—
when the new year arrives we will all
be a year older. By the Chinese account,

I am already in my fourth decade.
This morning my grandmother asked
for me by name. When my mother rang,

and I answered, my grandmother saw
my face, and smiled. My mother asked
her if she knew who I was. *Of course I do*,

my grandmother replied. *When are you coming
back?* she repeated, four times. *Next year*,
I replied. It is always next year. I am always

a year older by my own reckoning. I add,
and add, so afraid of subtracting.
What lies past zero? I do not wish to know.

# Count the Hours

We sit by the bed with its respirators
and monitors. My brother sketches the
many faces of our grandfather in charcoal.

At his fingertips, a language for making
sense of the world. My words would not arrive
for another twenty years. I stepped on and off

the scale; I ate a biscuit. Threw up lunch.
Ate an apple. Thirty laps of the pool.
Rinsing my costume in the bathroom sink,

riding the bus for an hour to the hospital.
He'd shaved his head of the silver mane
he'd been so proud of. We stood around him

and fanned him as he sweated. There was nothing
else we could do. He would die in this bed.
Afterwards, my grandmother dreamed of him.

She asked if he still smoked—he told her
*Of course. I'm already dead, aren't I?* We burned him
empty cartons of Marlboro Reds. The effigies

by his coffin silent and watching. Months later,
I find his gold-rimmed glasses in my drawer.
Eyes that no longer see are all-seeing.

My grandmother speaks to him now;
she is getting closer. I am, too—we all are.
My father and mother sleep and wake,

wake and sleep. We count the hours
and the days. The clock strikes one.
Trains pass through the station, without sound.

# The Call

*It is sweet. The heart dies of this sweetness.*
 'Song', Brigit Pegeen Kelly

I call my grandmother, and she remembers
my voice. She speaks my name, and it is full,
and whole. It rings in its clarity, its sounds

still formed by her lips. I hear her grind
her false teeth; she shifts her dentures repeatedly
around the inside of her mouth. *Have you eaten?*

I ask, and she says, *No. —Have you eaten?* I ask
again, because I forgot I had asked it. *Yes,*
she says. *Oh, good! What did you eat, Popo?*

Her clever hands would dip strips of fish
into flour, and drop them into hot oil.
Gold rings on her fingers. Her lilac nails.

I call my mother, and I tell her about it.
*Thank you for ringing my mother,* she says.
*She knew who I was,* I say. *That's good,* she replies,

then, *Will you go to the doctor with me tomorrow?*
I say, *No, I have to work.* My mother is quiet.
*We are all alone,* she says, at last. Once,

I put my head on her belly, and wondered
what it would be like to go back inside her.
Childish. Impossible. *Goodbye.* We both hang up.

# Ghazal for My Grandmother
*for Yeap Ah Choo*

I sing to you in the afternoons, grandmother.
I see you wear the ring I gave you, grandmother.

You have forgotten it was once mine. It fit
my finger perfectly, as it does yours, grandmother.

I hand you a book of photographs and poems. You turn
the pages restlessly—you never learned to read, grandmother.

When, and why were these pictures taken? Exactly
where are your memories hidden, grandmother?

The corridors are broken; the rooms are darkened.
Yet I look at you, and I behold you, grandmother.

On the shelf, in your Chinese dress and wavy hair,
you cradled your young son. Not yet a grandmother—

This morning, when I was absent, you told the world
I, little bell, love you best. My heart is yours, grandmother.

# Float

Hard to believe it was me who held her
in the water that day, the building's shadow long
over the shallow pool. *I won't let you sink—*

I placed one hand under her neck,
the other beneath her back, then slowly
pulled my hands away while she lay,

her face open to the sky. *Look, Popo,
you're floating!* Next: when to take in air,
how to push against the wet. Hard to believe

it'd been me in her arms, wrapped in muslin,
barely larger than a loaf of bread. It was her
in the afternoons, feeding me. The sun warm

that spring afternoon when we swam together
in the women's pool by the ocean. Salt in our eyes;
sea foam on our skins. Do ashes float, or sink?

We break the surface, breathe, and stroke
our way forward. Our bodies buoyant in the deep.
The waves parting, us gliding—tenacious, and alive.

# Spring Festival

The feeling begins in the stomach:
a stone pit swallowed by accident,
indigestible as homesickness.

My husband reminds me I write poems
in threes: three lines, three pathways.
One for the old life, one for the new

and one for the hours
I do not notice as they pass.
I bought twelve mandarins

on the new year's eve. On the first day
we took them to my parents' home.
My father gave me oranges and grapefruit

in return: I did not know why, or what
to do with them. On the second day,
I woke to the sun's rays across my face.

In the kitchen, my husband sliced
the fruit and squeezed each half.
He saved the pulp, added ginger,

then handed me a glass of bright juice.
It was sweet, and cold;
I consumed his love with greed.

Once, I watched a video of forty men
crouched around a concrete tank
brimming with water, holding a frame

larger than our apartment. To the count
of one voice, they hoist, dip, and lift;
they coax the white pulp to flow and settle

across a tightly stretched cloth mesh.
They move through a complex dance,
forearms sunk in liquid, feet marching

from tank to drying rack, and back again.
On the morning news, blonde children
speak Mandarin and write the character

for prosperity repeatedly, perfectly.
I reach for paper and ink, I mark this page,
I seek an address, I want to be delivered home.

## Paper Boats
*after Bing Xin*

They say the first year is for paper—
I have saved you all my poems.

The moon is full behind the clouds.
I fold each sheet along unseen lines.

Lengthwise, in half; here, a triangle.
Push, like this, and open it, carefully.

Little boats, with a shelter on each end.
What will stop them breaking on the rocks?

At the water, I bend and lower each
into the stream. The current takes hold at once.

The grass is flattened where I kneel.
Along the bank, the earth has turned to mud.

I follow each fragment as it floats
downriver. Words are heavy. Paper boats sink.

# The Hymen Diaries

# Seeking Heaven

*And in the hollow of my ink-stained palms*
*swallows will make their nest.*
'Reborn', Forugh Farrokhzad

This grass bed,
ringed by tussocks.
The snowmelt is receding.

Sweep of pebbles:
a broken wave,
milk-heavy breast.

A line of buried stones
punctuates the spine.
Dark mane, unbound.

Hands weighted
and open on emptied
sky-blue cloth, over full belly.

Press one ear to the ground—
storks cannot sing; can only clatter.

# Child

*after Andy Kissane's 'Joy and a Fibro Shack'*

Nearly midnight in the enclave
of apartments turned inwards,

blue light flickering in rooms.
A single wail, a drawn breath,

another scream—one long, continuous
keen. Teething, perhaps, or a fever.

Minutes after, a window is slammed
shut, but the crying persists. What

could be the matter? A child
is inconsolable; there is no reason

or solution. A mother, or a father,
holds her: a tethered, slapped boat.

# Woman, Crying

*So close to the end of my childbearing life*
*without children*
         'The Girl', Marie Howe

I sat in the café while your friend railed at me
—*if you knew you were going to leave why did you try,*
*and keep trying*—he meant for children, of course,

though we did not have them in the end.
Which comes first, blame or consequence?
I sat there, crying, while waitresses tiptoed

around me. One slipped me a napkin. I'd like
to go back. I'd like to have stood up, thrown water
in his face, smashed the plates onto the ground,

and yelled, *It's none of your fucking business!* I'd like
to have been the woman who made a scene. Instead,
I sat there and wept, unable to find the words

to say how I'd wanted to bear your children,
how much I'd loved you, and when each of them
failed to draw breath, how parts of me died, too.

# The Numbers Game

In the morning room you offer up your arm—
a tight band, several squeezes of the hand,
a pinprick, release. The nurse will call later

with the results. We are looking for a trend;
we want to keep it within a range. Lie back,
insert the wand, watch the sonogram. Today,

the friendly technician is also an artist.
She tells you, *I make sculptures*, and you ask if
they resemble ovaries. She is surprised, then

she says, *Yes*. It's not rocket science: what goes in,
comes out. Your follicles are growing; at the right time,
inject this. Your eggs will ripen. Twelve hours later

the doctor will insert a needle through the wall
of your uterus, and harvest them. A scientist
will be present; he will scan the fluid in the test-tubes

through a microscope, right there in the room.
We count them together: there is certainty in numbers.
*All you need is one*, but the game is an upside-down

pyramid. Ten eggs, but not all are ripe; not all ripe
eggs fertilise; not all fertilised eggs continue to grow.
Divide and conquer. If there is, indeed, a blastocyst,

then we transfer. Now the long wait. Not all embryos implant. The blood test is 99% accurate, but the stain in your underwear does not lie. A single red butterfly.

# Emilia

Her eyes (still grey, blue, and green) search
mine out. I meet her gaze, then hold her.

She bobs her head at me, and I lower mine
in return. Our foreheads meet and cleave.

I tilt her backwards, my hand cradling her neck,
then lift her towards me, and tilt her again.

She clings to me—freedom and safety,
safety and freedom. It is a game she knows,

and she smiles, and smiles. Her laughter,
a talisman; her eyes, a ward. She sees me,

and so I exist. I am here, and I suffer.
Soon she will go, and my love with her.

I wake to the smell of milk. The hungry
mouth. The animal grip of her clenched fists.

# Borrowed

*after Kendra DeColo's 'Playlist: 11 Weeks'*

What does it mean, then, to never
be able to write: *that was the night*
*she was conceived*, and be truthful?

Everything has been truncated.
Before, I could pretend: a fallow
period, a recovery, a choice.

Taken from me, from this broken body.
Strength of a stag beetle lifting
hundreds of times its own weight.

Iridescent, glossy like oil rubbed
into a pregnant body I have never
occupied. I have the wounds to show

for it. I am marked, of some other coven:
women who steal babies for as long as they can.
Only borrowed. Never ours to bring home.

# Whole

It is winter, and we have just made love.
All throughout, I knew it was the last time
we would lie together intact. Tomorrow:

the bright lights of the operating theatre.
The anaesthetist will lay his cool hands
on my skin, inject his drug, and take

me under. The surgeon will make
four little cuts, and a final, larger one.
When he is done, I will be put together

again. My soul will find my body,
and my body will wake. I remember
the pain from before, except this time,

it will be worse. I think of the woman
at the temple of monkeys. How softly
she spoke. How she told me

to stay: she would feed me rice and fruit.
A girl blessed me with holy ash; I startled
at her touch on my face. The sound of coins

in her small hands. You cried out as you came,
a declaration of the living. Our quickened breaths
slowing even as I rose, feet bare on the floor.

# Tether

Afterwards, I wiped myself,
and there was blood. Not like
the torrent of before, cramping
and pouring out, the hot rush

of thick red, dark clots sunk
to the bottom. That is all behind
me now, because I said the words.
*Do it. It's my body*—

The doctor signed the papers
only after he spoke to my husband,
the shadows of his children dark
in the room. I think of their births:

I am in the delivery suite, though
I do not know the woman
bearing down, screaming,
the first wife of my husband.

Blood dries up and goes away.
I walk around without a tether.
A mother crosses my path. Her child kicks
a ball over the grass. I simply move aside.

# Prince of Wales Hospital, July 2018
*after Frida Kahlo's* Henry Ford Hospital (The Flying Bed), *1932*

At six o'clock in the morning, two women
wiped down my body in bed because I could not
stand without passing out. They did it tenderly,
like I was their sister, or mother, or daughter.

One put a dry hand on my forehead as I wept.
*I'm so sorry,* she told me, over and over. *It's okay,*
I said, as I cried. There are no babies in this bed,
no snails, no cast-gold hips. The flowers have not yet

arrived in their pot, with the bright label *cyclamen.*
Around and around we go in this place. I walk
along the corridor towards the light, then back up,
away from it. H is for helicopter; H is for hospital.

Last night, it rained: a dark stain left on the driveway.
The nurse this morning had been named for a waterlily.
She looked at me sharply when I said it. *How
do you know that? —I'm a writer,* I said. Her face

softened. It was my business to know this.
It was hers to dole out pills in small cups.
I take my tablets. The pain swells and ebbs.
The doctor comes, freshly combed. Yesterday,

he delivered four babies. *You can go home
tomorrow.* Can I? Go home? Tomorrow—

# The Hymen Diaries

I

Stone in fist. Rock in hand.
Sand a canvas, moon not yet—

circle of circles. There an angle,
here a curve—at the centre, only

your own hewn face. Spiral of nothing.
The tide comes. Takes it all—

II

You turn the corner into an entire room
of uteri—watercoloured wombs on wallpaper,
stitched and stuffed fabric fallopian tubes

casting solid shadows. A sumi ink landscape
of breasts, rising and falling, peaks and troughs,
valleys and mountains. Here, a jagged skull:

memento mori, the jaw missing, eyeholes
dark like the void. A great big fuck-you
to fertility. Suddenly, you don't feel so alone.

III

Almost transgressive to look at the woman
with her legs slightly parted. Not a woman,
but knowing a woman had to pose for it.
Every fold of skin, every minute hair, present—

A toddler covers her eyes when she sees it.
Her mother leads her around to the front
and waits for her to look again. They talk,
quietly, so I can only imagine the wise, open

conversation I never had. Pubis, vulva, labia,
clitoris. The stomach flat, the hips concave.
Pert breasts, blush of nipples. I have never
looked like this, not even in my dreams.


IV

She has clamped a hand over her mouth.
She has two children standing next to her.
She has stopped painting figures.
Black, rust, white—concatenation
of snow and rain. To exist is to resist.

# Griefs

# Griefs

难过: a difficult crossing

I watched you climb the fence,
hoisting yourself up and swinging
a leg over, knowing where to place
your foot, the other leg home free—

you, waiting for me, watching,
knowing it was impossible
for me to pull myself up and over
the way you did, so fluidly—

splinters raked in my palm,
which my skin would grow over,
and we turned to see him lift the latch
and walk straight through the gate—

困难: a tree in the mouth

I have not spoken to you in months,
not since the words tumbled out
broken. Unlike sea glass, the shards
are brittle, even as they glitter, a hand

full of cut diamonds. Words fall apart
like salt spray after a wave breaks
open on the cliffs by the ocean.
We are looking at each other

from our vantage points.
You endure the same losses even
as I tread the path you assiduously
turn from. Here, I walk alone.


过去: crossed over, gone

We meet for a meal, hungry ghosts
mouthing food they can smell
but not digest. We say nothing.
There is nothing left to say.

The past is called bygones:
by the by we are all gone
when we cross each other out.
Why do we recall what split us open?

Slipping from our skins
like boiled chickens
trussed up naked. Dripping juices
are always stained with blood.

# Paper Tiger

画虎画皮难画骨，知人知面不知心。

*When you draw a tiger, you draw its skin, but not its bones.*
*When you know a person, you know their face, but not their heart.*

Chinese proverb

To walk into a lair, knowing—
prey are attuned to every move.

With each muscular threat, fear ripples.
I know how to hide in the long grass.

The shadows grow and fall around us;
we all thirst for the same waterhole.

In the night, nocturnal eyes reflect truth.
The dark covers the migration of innocent mice.

In the morning light, your skin is paper:
you are tearing at the seams. Your stripes

are the remnants of a long-held cruelty.
Give it up. Eat. Drink. Rest. Stop hurting.

# The Wall

*Even / the apples were poison.*
                    'A Unified Berlin', Ann Townsend

The fruit hangs low, russet and ripe,
the trunk grown thick on the other side.

What's yours is yours: there is no mine.
My roots will not slake your thirst.

The sky, cerulean; the sea, wine-dark.
Your eyes are open, but you are blind.

We hunger—we bite. You devour the harvest.
I spit out my mouthful: bitter, and rotten.

Better to starve. Become smaller and smaller.
Fruit by fruit: the wall festers. Decomposes.

# Rot

*but I can't stop my distress at …*
*their rank indifference if the carcase*
*in the dirt is stallion, child, or rabid dog.*
                    'Vultures', Judith Beveridge

Why do we call them birds of prey?
Raptor, from *rapio*: to seize or take
by force. She didn't cry when she told me

how close it was to rape. I've been there:
I've denied the danger, thought, *You're making it up*—
until the violence happens; and you're not.

The scavenger, an archer—a stalker in the grass.
He hits his mark until it ceases to move.
I went limp; I played dead. I meant to survive.

Predator, plunderer—your unending hunger;
your naked wattle, coated in carrion, will rot.

# Firmament

*I notice the ones in pain*
*shine more than the others.*
       'Nights in the Neighborhood', Linda Gregg

Walking home alone after dinner,
the shadowed streets menace.
There are no stars in the firmament.

Your hand reaches from the darkness
and closes around my throat—the twisting cat
outlined in air before gravity takes hold.

★

One foot in front of the other: follow
the ribbon of road. At home, in the top
drawer: a box of matches. Struck sulphur—

incandescent phosphorus. Who first said
*there is no smoke without fire?* You've taken
all my oxygen. There is nothing left to burn.

# Season

In a long box at the flower market:
                        bunches of pink peonies.

When you left, he said
                        he'd never buy them again.

The glass is thin around his apartment;
                        the vases are full of new blooms.

# Looking Glass

My grandmother taught me to always leave
the house well-groomed. *You never know
whom you might see.* Today, sitting down

to lunch, I looked up, to my left. Beyond
the glass: a woman, walking briskly, staring
right at me. Our eyes met briefly. She knew

who I was. She knew that I knew who
she was. I told my friend—too late.
She was gone. It had no consequence.

I went to the bathroom and checked myself.
Red lipstick, hair streaked with grey, cheeks
flushed from the fire. Alive, and free.

She: a dark-haired, sharp-eyed sprite. Perhaps
the window, from the outside, was just a mirror—
perhaps she saw not me, but a cold, windblown wife.

# After

And yet there are new shoots growing
from the bamboo in the sunshine
and the cat is warming himself on the pavers.

The violets are ankle-deep and three snails
have left their silver trails across the path where
they exited the denseness to get where they were

going. The neighbour's traps in the back lane
have caught nothing; last month I opened the gate
so a rat could scurry out while the cats watched,

bewildered. A man writes *a woman in ecstasy*
*or terror* and I fling the paper across the room
because he doesn't know or care—

every place we look a man traverses a country
littered with bodies. I want to plant signs that say
*here was April, here was May, here was June* ...

They use the passive and try to erase us. A voice
breaks the silence but they tell us *we are all*
*human, we are flawed, there is nothing we can do.* No-one

is asking for perfection—just courage. We've lit
the fire. Come out of the cave. Listen: believe us.
We survived. We have nothing left to lose.

# The Walk

*'I like to go to the ends of things—'* Bella Li

The day we first met, we walked through
the city, across a bridge, around gardens,
inside galleries. We sat outdoors
in the shade, and I watched the fountain

while you went for coffee. A bird swooped, landed,
and searched for crumbs. Later, we followed the length
of the river, and you said you were writing about lakes.
I took a photo of you looking up at the arching bamboo.

By the dock, the *Carpentaria* was crimson, and anchored;
the sky opened, and it rained. We did not speak
much; we shared an easy silence. I told you of the end
of Australia, at Byron Bay. You told me not to jump.

# Content

*tell yourself that anytime now*
*we will rise and walk away*
*from somebody else's life.*
        'A Dream of Foxes', Lucille Clifton

Always the water falling
into the pond below, fish
with their mouths open,
hungry circles below the surface.

The sky wide blue and broken,
air thrumming with cricketsong
rising and falling—halting
abruptly, the silence filled

with bird cries and the low groan
of a man in pain or in love.
Midafternoons like these,
you cannot imagine the life

you left behind, all marble
and leather, gilt mirrors and gold.
These days, there are metal tools,
sweat, and our tireless

hands. Moving to make room
for the other, the giving up of dead
things, taking into our selves only
what we've earned, and what is sweet.

# Sweet Truth

# Sweet Truth

*after Wendy Morrison's Salt, 2017*

I push a fingertip along the rail:
salt. My hair stiff and obedient

in the weighted air. Salt blooms
within the kiln. It eats away at steel.

The long march. The spinning wheel.
The wife who looked: a crystal

pillar. Blocks of currency dissolving.
Rake the ponds of salt, let them shrivel

for the harvest. Pink like a stain that won't
come clear. The magic salt grinder

fallen from the captain's ship, sunk to the
bottom of a sea. Were it so simple, this

knowledge that we are all but salt.
Sweat and tears. Sweet truth.

# Making Sense

*I will remain a small book*
*hidden away deep*
*in the library.*
        'Red with a Touch of Sulfur', Zubair Ahmed

I tell my students:
poetry is a way to make sense
of what you fear.

I sing to them of
blackbirds. I read my poems
aloud. I am without shell.

I walk to the station:
faceless, every passerby
a universe, oblivious.

The grocer stacks oranges;
the cashier rubs plastic
between finger and thumb;

children recite their
times tables: do they all
mark the stars as they fall?

The hollowed-out train
on a winter afternoon. Shadows
of trees and buildings flicker past.

A girl at her desk begins a poem:
I dreamed everyone, even my own
mother, had forgotten my name—

# Giving Up

*They are like Snow White. They just fall away from the world.*
Elisabeth Hultcrantz

The young women breathe,
but their hands, if lifted
then released, only flop

like broken wings. Beneath
their closed lids, they stare
like the dead, unseeing.

Once, they bit into apples,
and spat out the worms.
Juice ran down their chins.

Their hair thickens and curls.
Their breasts have budded
in their long, unsettled sleep.

One day, they cried out,
then collapsed. They will not
wake; they do not hear or speak.

They are in glass coffins.
Outside, the water rises
and presses on the panes.

The children know that
if they blink or move they'll
drown all over again.

# Needle

*But her end is bitter as wormwood, sharp as a two-edged sword.*
Proverbs 5:4

She lifts amber to her lips
and speaks of roses and light.
Eyes broken as kaleidoscopes,
history spliced and repeating—

a torrent: pain like a forest
sprung from needles tossed
from a basket. Tangled threads
glisten and vibrate, taut as webs.

Listen: we can hear the fiddlers,
urgent at their strings. The wind
will carry music across the water.
The river has worn a hole clean

through the stone's heart. Every
drop relentless, hungry for the sea.

# Sewing Daisies
*after Mary Shelley's Frankenstein*

We lay out strips and squares of linen and I think of a shroud—
how long after a person ceases to be does the heart
forget to beat? I sit in the sunlight and mark out my patterns:

today we are embroidering daisies, for spring. I think of the flowers
that push up from burial mounds before grass even takes root.
Petals white as the knuckles of body-snatchers, I plan

where to make my cuts, which organs to remove, what parts
I will stitch together so finely the gaps cannot be seen. I have heard
of electricity, of a jolt of power so sudden it can take life, or ignite.

My fingers fly across the cloth. Stalks carpet the edge.
What does a man most want, if not a woman, or a child?
Did God make man in His own image? What, then, will man create?

The sun has set, and the gaslights are lit. Tendrils of green leaves
curling like disease. My needle stabs my finger: it hurts, and I bleed.

# Maria-Mercè in the Palm Grove

I am dreaming: we are in the palm grove.
It is night—the stars are present in the cloudless sky.
I am free from pain. We walk in the garden,
past the tiled fountain with its trickled song.

I come to the tree, and we stop. I place my hand,
the one that writes, onto its trunk. In the dark
I can feel where it divided into three: to live
once is not enough. One is born, one must fight,

one will die. You ask me the questions. I say,
*Yes, yes,* and *yes.* You give me the wine in its ewer.
It is good wine. I am pouring it slowly over the roots;
I am washing each stem, staining my hands and feet crimson.

It is done. Now the tree is mine. I will eat its sweet dates
every harvest. My body has become a sickly flower, rotting fruit.
I am waiting to return, to become a palm, a tree.
Our shadows are tongues, restless on the dry earth.

# The Road

*for Daisy Cassidy*

The morning light in long lines
through the windowpane. A girl

in a pink jacket coming down the road.
Her pale hair, a river. Her eyes,

two chips of sky. Warm hands
and stolen time. Home is no

sanctuary. The bed delivers no dreams.
Take this road to the very end—

low clouds point the way.
Love buoyant as a ferry

crossing to the mainland. The sea
changes names. Shadows blanket half the earth.

A father walks his daughter to school.
He kisses her goodbye. The rain turns into snow.

# The Dome

*the eyes like birds took off to free skies,*
*and so they stayed yearning for space.*
                    Elisaveta Bagryana

Silver service under the dome—*this was a bank,*
our auntie told us. *I used to work here.* None
of us belong here: not me, not you, not the waiters

in their starched suits and polished shoes.
The tea is hot. The juice is sweet and cold.
By the time our meals arrive, all of us are hungry.

In between mouthfuls, we talk about everything
and nothing. We are still strangers, and our lives
are unexplored rooms in the dark. A spark flies

as I kindle a flame. I ask the young man for a name
of a poet from his homeland. He fumbles; he forgets
his English, remembering only the language of his birth.

We have all come carrying branches in our hands.
They are sticks, or parts of a nest. Our hearts catch fire.
I watch your eyes, so like your father's—the blue of open skies.

# Furrow

*All the rivers run into the sea; yet the sea is not full;*
*unto the place from whence the rivers come, thither they return again.*
                                                        Ecclesiastes 1:7

*Scotland, like a dream*, you wrote. *Did it really happen?*
Yet today I listened to a writer speak about his book
set on the Isle of Lewis. The producer had recorded

the howling of the wind and the cries of the birds.
The interviewer said the skin of the earth was thin
in this place; the water, nearly phosphorescent in the moonlight.

I think of you, Eric, in the hunting lodge at Uig—
sun sets over sands, shadows deepen into velvet.
Are you speaking in Gaelic? The church pews are empty.

There are no psalms being uttered in that hall.
It was low tide when I crossed the stream and walked
the face of the hill. The grass, a restless sea in the night.

Why did you go back? *I'm a loser, that's why.*
That final morning, I sang to you, my voice
rising up the stair. Even the hung skulls listened. No-one
loses anything. We all leave so we can come home.

# Farm Work

*for Anna Kerdjik Nicholson and Joost Kerdjik*

I

nearly dusk when we arrive. earth
billows behind the car along the track.
fingers remember how to unlatch
the gate—brittle metal like frost on grass.

II

the sun sets on the horizon, treacle
over treeline. a mob of kangaroo,
bounding to the left and away over
the fence. slow, grey dots of sheep.

III

in the tree's heart, an aboriginal
stone—blade or axe head, a human tool.
smooth as a pebble. shaped by a hand,
used by a mind. time like blown dust.

IV

a burial mound, dust to dust—
i think of flowers on a grave.
here, the topsoil, skirts loosened
across grass when the wind blows.


V

no rain for days—today we're laying
pipes. jarring music of the tractor
dredging furrows back and forth.
there, a rock we cleaved clean in half.


VI

hot, strong tea, and shortbread.
the afternoon sun in striations
on the rug. the tulips grow
and bloom, despite having been cut.


VII

not much to do at night besides
gather by the fire. we feed, we rest.
the dog is curled up. he dreams.
outside, the stars are unknowable.

# Loom

*after Tina Kane's 'Time Watch'*

The first time I met you, Tina, was
the last time. Those were scant days,
snatched minutes between readings.

You held my hand, Tina, and pressed it
to his; you looked from his face to mine,
and back to his. I looked down at your ring—

an opal, a universe encased in gold,
drawing the eye to your clever hands
that once pulled magic from thin air.

In the stone-walled chamber at Stirling Castle
we lifted our eyes to seven hung tapestries:
the hunt of the unicorn. The pomegranates

on its borders swelled ripe with months.
I fingered the loom, and imagined the flight
of the shuttle, the dance of your fingers,

your bright, watchful eyes. Thread by thread,
warp by weft, you kept weaving—did you know
what your life would look like at the very end?

The loom is quiet; its work is now complete.
I feel the weight of your spirit,
pull the memory over me, a blanket of light.

# Turning the Bend

*... We all ache for an off-button — but turn*
*the bend and everything quietens ...*
        'Walking in the Reserve', Judith Beveridge

I wake in the night to the roar of my thoughts.
I think of what you might say.

Sometimes I go to your poems, and there
it is, clear as day: proof that you, too, have turned

these questions over in your mind; have offered
up the answers. You move deliberately, your feet

placed carefully, so as to not trample a living
creature. The truth is, I want to be still: like

the artist who takes a photograph of a single
bloomed rose, year after year. There is merit

in quietude, in the precise layering of sound,
image, and object. In the simple acts of walking,

waiting, and witnessing. And the heart, a mystery—
brimming with sweetness, with kindness, with love.

# Cycle

We cycle to the end of the road
as the sun sinks behind the hill.
Cars turn on their headlights;

they surge past us in a rush.
A single line separates our bodies
from those bodies of steel,

of certain death. We pump
our legs up and down; our hands
grip firm on the bars. It's getting dark

when his tail lights up and winks.
My head replies: I'm following.

★

My head replies: I'm following;
my heart is leading this dance.
A flock of white birds bisects

the cloudless sky, which means
it will be cold—no blanket
to stop the day's heat from escaping.

I wait for the pot to boil. The recipe I follow
says to reduce the liquid to half its volume,
but I forgot how salt can concentrate.

The meat is falling off the bones.
I watch him mouth every last rib.

★

I watch him mouth every last rib;
he begins at my throat, circles my breasts,
then moves to my belly. I part my legs,

and he kisses me there. I think
of the first boy. I think of how he gagged.
I'd shut the curtains earlier, but left

the lamps burning. I no longer have room
for shame. Skin and bodies. He returns
his lips to mine, and I taste my own sweetness.

We give of ourselves, over and over.
I forget how quietness sounds.

★

I forget how quietness sounds.
The washing machine is an aeroplane
ascending. The fridge beeps sharply

when its door is left unshut. The kettle
roils its fury; the dishwasher moans
and sighs. The thermostat judges,

and clicks the stove ring into red.
Smoke rises. The alarm screams.
I lower and lid the heavy pan.

The oven murmurs its loss
long after dinner is over.

★

Long after dinner is over,
my father is still cleaning the kitchen.
He likes to mop the floor.

In our previous apartment, he would pour
buckets of water onto the tiles,
and scrub them with a stiff broom.

From over here, he looks like
an ancient boatman with his pole,
far from the nearest river bank.

His bark raincoat is discarded;
his bare skin gleams with sweat.

★

His bare skin gleams with sweat
as he builds my bicycle from parts.
I watch his hands assemble the frame,

tighten the wheels, adjust the brakes.
He fits the saddle. I haven't ridden
in years. I swing my right leg up

and over; I wobble down
the corridor, surprised how fast
I go. I remember how to brake.

He holds the gate open, and we're off.
We will cycle to the end of the road.

# Notes

'忍' means 'to endure'. The word comprises the character for 'knife' 刀, 'heart' 心, and a mark that stands in for the character for 'droplet', 点, indicating a drop of blood.

'A Thousand Crimson Blooms' contains an epigraph from 'Don't Trample This Flower' by Bing Xin, reprinted with kind permission from McGill-Queen's University Press. Blatt, Herbert. 2016. 'Don't Trample This Flower.' In *The Flowering of Modern Chinese Poetry*. Montreal, Quebec: MQUP, p. 64.

'Courage' contains the phrase 吓到了, which literally means 'fright arrived'—the arrival of fright. The word for 'fright' comprises the characters for 'mouth' 口 and 'down' 下, making the line 'a downturned mouth'.

'Fortune-Telling' contains an epigraph from 'Signs' from *The Selected Levis* by Larry Levis, selected by David St. John, © 2000. Reprinted by permission of the University of Pittsburgh Press.

'The Call' contains an epigraph by Brigit Pegeen Kelly, excerpt from 'Song' from *Song*. Copyright © 1995 by Brigit Pegeen Kelly. Reprinted with the permission of The Permissions Company, LLC on behalf of BOA Editions Ltd., boaeditions.org.

'Seeking Heaven' contains an epigraph by Forugh Farrokhzad, excerpt from 'Reborn' from *Sin: Selected poems*

'The Hymen Diaries' is a response, in parts, to the following artworks:

I: after Katie Griesar's *Everything changes, nothing is lost* (2014), site-specific installation at Long Cove Point, Maine, USA, seen on the artist's page at https://www. flickr.com/photos/9610116@N02/14207511879; photo posted on 7 June 2014.

II: after Annette Messager's *Papier peint Utérus (Wallpaper Uterus)* (2017) and *Utérus doigt d'honneur (Uterus Giving the Finger)* (2017), seen at *Pudique-publique*, Institut Valencià d'Art Modern, 5 July to 4 November 2018, Valencia, Spain.

III: after Paul McCarthy's *That Girl (T.G. Awake)* (2012–13), seen at *Hyper Real*, National Gallery of Australia, 20 October 2017 to 18 February 2018, Canberra, Australia.

IV: after Juana Francés's *Silenci* (1953) and *Dona am dos xiquets* (1952), seen at *A Contratemps: Mig segle d'artistes valencianes (1929–1980)*, Institut Valencià d'Art Modern, 28 April to 2 September 2018, Valencia, Spain, and *Cometos* (1989), seen at Museo de Arte Contemporáneo de Alicante, permanent collection, Alicante, Spain.

'Griefs' contains the following characters, translated here:
难过 : sadness, grief
困难 : difficulty, obstacle
过去 : the past, what has passed

'The Wall' contains an epigraph from Ann Townsend's 'A Unified Berlin', reprinted with kind permission of the author. This poem originally appeared on poets.org, published by the Academy of American Poets, on 8 March 2019.

'Rot' contains an epigraph from Judith Beveridge's 'Vultures', reprinted with kind permission of the author. An earlier version of this poem appeared in *Meanjin*, Autumn 2019.

'Firmament' contains an epigraph by Linda Gregg, excerpt from 'Nights in the Neighborhood' from *The Sacraments of Desire*. Copyright © 1991 by Linda Gregg. Reprinted with the permission of The Permissions Company, LLC on behalf of Graywolf Press, Minneapolis, Minnesota, graywolfpress.org.

'The Walk' contains an epigraph spoken by Bella Li to the author on the day of their walk together in Brisbane, Queensland, in August 2017.

'Content' contains an epigraph by Lucille Clifton, excerpt from 'A Dream of Foxes' from *The Collected Poems of Lucille Clifton 1965–2010*. Copyright © 1996 by Lucille Clifton. Reprinted with the permission of The Permissions Company, LLC on behalf of BOA Editions Ltd., boaeditions.org.

'Making Sense' contains an epigraph from Zubair Ahmed's poem 'Red with a Touch of Sulfur', which appeared online at poets.org, published by the Academy of American Poets, on 20 May 2019.

'Giving Up' was inspired by the photograph by Magnus Wennman of two Roma girls, Djeneta and Ibadeta, who are refugees from Kosovo living in Sweden. Djeneta and Ibadeta suffer from *uppgivenhetssyndrom*, or resignation syndrome, a condition that exists among refugees in Sweden, whereby children of asylum seekers withdraw from the world, becoming completely physically non-responsive. The quote in the epigraph from Elisabeth Hultcrantz, a doctor who treats these children, was taken from an essay by Rachel Aviv, 'The Trauma of Facing Deportation', published in *The New Yorker* on 27 March 2017. The metaphor for the glass coffin in my poem was in part derived from the experience of Georgi, a sufferer of the syndrome, as detailed in the same article.

'Needle' contains an epigraph from *The Holy Bible, King James Version*. Cambridge Edition: 1769; *King James Bible Online*, 2020. www.kingjamesbibleonline.org.

'Maria-Mercè in the Palm Grove' is an imagining of the Catalonian poet Maria-Mercè Marçal in the Palmeral of Elche, Alicante, Spain. The poem also owes a debt to the late poet WS Merwin, for his activism replanting palms on the island of Maui in Hawaii, and to his poem, 'Palm'.

'The Dome' contains an epigraph from 'The Bird with the Engine Heart' by Elisaveta Bagryana, translated from the Bulgarian by Brenda Walker with Valentine Borrisov and Beline Tonchev, published by Forest Books in 1993, reprinted with kind permission from Forest Books.

'Furrow' contains an epigraph from *The Holy Bible, King James Version*. Cambridge Edition: 1769; *King James Bible Online*, 2020. www.kingjamesbibleonline.org. The poem also references the BBC's *Scotland Outdoors* podcast, 'Peter May on Lewis', 26 September 2018.

'Turning the Bend' contains an epigraph from 'Walking in the Reserve' by Judith Beveridge, published in *Sun Music: New and selected poems*, Giramondo, 2018.

# Acknowledgements

I would like to acknowledge that I live and work on unceded Aboriginal land of the Gadigal people of the Eora Nation. I pay my respects to their elders past, present, and emerging.

My deepest thanks go to my publisher, Aviva Tuffield, and my editor, Judith Bishop, without whom this book would not have come into being.

My gratitude, as always, to my parents, and my parents-in-law, for their support, care, and love. To my husband, Colin, who is my anchor, and who continues to believe in and support my writing.

My thanks, also, to the editors of the following journals in which some of these poems have previously appeared, at times in different forms:

*Antipodes, The Margins, The Australian, Australian Poetry Journal, Cease, Cows, Cha, Cordite, Djed Press, The Enchanting Verses, Glasgow Review of Books, Island, The Lifted Brow, Meanjin, Overland, Peril, Sijo, Stilts, Victorian Women's Trust,* and *Voice and Verse.*

Several of the poems in this collection were previously published in the chapbook *Dark Matter* (2018), from Recent Work Press, in conjunction with the International Poetry Studies Institute in Canberra.

'A Thousand Crimson Blooms' (originally published as 'A Thousand Blooms') and 'Seeking Heaven' were commissioned by *Peril Magazine* as response poems to the artwork of Vipoo Srivilasa and Sofi Basseghi respectively, collected in the exhibition *Hyphenated* at the SUBSTATION in 2018.

'The Numbers Game' was highly commended in the inaugural Quantum Words Science Poetry Competition 2018.

'Firmament' was commissioned for *Giant Steps: Fifty poets reflect on the Apollo 11 moon landing and beyond* (2019), edited by Paul Munden and Shane Strange, and published by Recent Work Press in Canberra.

'Content' was longlisted for the University of Canberra Vice-Chancellor's International Poetry Prize 2019.